1. Prologue

THERE is perhaps nothing extraordinary in the fact that man is wise and just, takes great care to provide for his own children, -shows due consideration for his parents, seeks sustenance for himself, protects himself against plots, and possesses all the other gifts of nature which are his. For man has been endowed with speech, of all things the most precious, and has been granted reason, which is of the greatest help and use.

Moreover, he knows how to reverence and worship the gods. But that dumb animals should by nature possess some good quality and should have many of man's amazing excellences assigned to them along with man, is indeed a remarkable fact. And to know accurately the special characteristics of each, and how living creatures also have been a source of interest no less than man, demands a trained intelligence and much learning. Now I am well aware of the labour that others have expended on this subject, yet I have collected all the materials that I could; I have clothed them in untechnical language, and am persuaded that my achievement is a treasure far from negligible. So if anyone considers them profitable, let him make use of them; anyone who does not consider them so may give them to his father to keep and attend to.

For not all things give pleasure to all men, nor do all men consider all subjects worthy of study. Although I was born later than many accomplished writers of an earlier day, the accident of date ought not to mulct me of praise, if I too produce a learned work whose ampler research and whose choice of language make it deserving of serious attention.

Mythology, mariners' yarns, vulgar superstitions, the ascertained facts of nature — all serve to adorn a tale and, on occasion, to point a moral. His religion is the popular stoicism of the age. Aleian repeatedly affirms his belief in the gods and in divine providence; the wisdom and beneficence of Nature are held up to veneration; the folly and selfishness of man are contrasted with the untaught virtues of the animal world. Some animals, to be sure, have their failings, but he chooses rather to dwell upon their good qualities, devotion, courage, self-sacrifice, gratitude. Again, animals are guided by reason, and from them we may learn contentment, control of the passions, and calm in the face of death.

2. The Lion in old age

When the Lion is advanced in years and heavy with age he is quite incapable of hunting and is glad to take his ease in caves or lairs in the jungle; nor has he the spirit to attack even the weakest of animals, for he mistrusts his age and is conscious of his bodily infirmity.

Whereas his offspring confident in the vigour of their youth and their natural strength go out to hunt and bring the old one with them by pushing him along. Then, when they have come half the necessary distance, they leave him behind and give themselves to the chase.

And when they have obtained enough for themselves and for their sire, with a magnificent and thrilling roar, even as banqueters summon a guest, so do these young children summon their aged father to the feast.

And he comes softly, step by step, and almost crawling, and embraces his children, fawning upon them a little with his tongue as though he applauded their success, and attacks the meal and feasts with his sons. This is no order of Solon's to the Lions: it is Nature that teaches them-Nature that reeks naught of laws made by man. But she is a law that does not change.

3. The Eagle's Feathers

Not only when he is alive and active do birds dread the Eagle, the king of birds, and cower down when he appears, but if one mixes his feathers with those of other birds, the Eagle's remain entire and untainted, while the others, unable to endure the association, rot away.

The Mouse
Mice, besides being prolific creatures, bring forth many offspring at a single birth; and if by some means they happen to eat salt, then they bring forth a great number and far more than is customary.

4. The Crocodile and its young

And when Crocodiles give birth they test the legitimate and the bastard offspring in this manner. If on being hatched a young Crocodile immediately seizes something, it is henceforward reckoned among the family and is loved by its parents, is believed to be, and is counted as, one of the Crocodiles.

If however it remains inactive and is lazy and fails to seize some fly or gnat or earthworm or young lizard, the sire tears it to pieces as a poor creature, spurious, and no kin of his. And as these creatures act, even so do Eagles appear to test their legitimate offspring by the rays of the sun and to love them as the result of judgment and not of any feeling.

The Asp, its fangs

I have heard that the Asp's fangs, which one would be correct in styling 'poison — carriers,' -have an exceedingly thin coating, so to say, round them, like membrane, covering them all over. So when the Asp fastens its mouth on a man, they say that these membranes part and the poison is ejected, and then again they close and unite.

The Scorpion, its sting

Again, the sting of the Scorpion has a kind of hollow core, so very fine as to be hardly visible. That is where they say the poison resides and is engendered, and directly the Scorpion strikes, the poison shoots forward along the sting and flows out.

And this opening also, through which it passes, is so fine as to be invisible to the eye. But if a man spits upon it the sting is blunted and numbed and becomes incapable of wounding.

Puppies

Even if a Bitch produces a number of puppies, it is nevertheless the one that issues first from the womb and the eldest of the litter that declares the sire.

At any rate it bears the closest resemblance to him in every respect, while the rest are born as chance may dictate. In this matter Nature appears to pursue reason in setting the male which sows above the female which receives.

5. The Moon, its influence on shellfish and Animals

Here is another characteristic of Testaceans and Crustaceans.
As the moon wanes they are in the habit of somehow
becoming both emptier and lighter. Among Testaceans the
purple Shellfish, whelks, red thorny oysters, and those of the
same species prove my statement; among Crustaceans, edible
crabs, crayfish, lobsters, crabs in general, and all their kin.
It is also asserted that the young of beasts of burden born
when the moon is on the wane are less capable and feebler
than others, and what is more, those who have knowledge of
these matters recommend that animals born in this part of the
month should not be reared on the ground that they are not of
good quality. Whereas animals born at the new moon, as I
learn, either utter their natural sound or drop. The Lion alone,
as Aristotle says, does neither.

6. The Basse and its otolith

Aristotle asserts that the Basse is extremely quick of hearing, and so too are the Chromis, the Saupe, and the Mullet. I have ascertained also that the Basse knows full well that there is in fact a small stone in its head, and this in winter becomes intensely cold and causes it severe pain.
This is why at that season of the year it warms itself and devises this highly effective remedy against the cold due to the stone. And the Chromis, the Sea-bream, and the Maigre, I learn, do the same, for these fish also have a similar stone.

Fishes and their 'parasites'

It seems that among fishes also there exist parasites! At any rate the Sucking-fish, as it is called, nibbles what the dolphin catches, and the dolphin is glad that he should, and willingly allows him a share. That is Why the fish is exceedingly plump, like one gorged with a rich and abundant feast.

And Theron in Menander's play boasts that he has led men by the nose and used them as his manger. And Cleisophus covered one of his eyes with a bandage out of compliment to Philip who had lost an eye at the siege of Methone. Sucking-fish and dolphin are in my opinion friends and messmates, for whereas man understands flattery like other vices, brute beasts do not.

7. The Elephant and its young

Here again is an example of the Elephant's strong affection for its young. Elephant-hunters dig trenches and these animals fall into them, and while some are captured, others are killed. You will learn from other sources how they dig these trenches, how they are shaped, how deep, and what the entrances to them are like. I however propose to reveal and demonstrate the Elephants affection.

When the mother sees her young one has fallen into one of the trenches, she does not hesitate, does not waste time, but rushing up at full speed, all courage and passion, hurls herself upon the head of her child, and the pair meet one and the same end, for the young one is crushed by the mother's weight; she falls on her head . . . So those who doubt whether Elephants have a natural affection for their offspring are absurd.

8. The Seal

Seals give birth on land, but by degrees lead their cubs down to the water and give them a taste of the sea.

Then they lead them back to the original place of their birth, and again bring them down to the sea, and quickly lead them out, and by doing this many times they end by making them excellent swimmers.

And they easily slide into life in the sea: their instruction affords an inducement, while Nature forces them to love the haunts and the habits of their mothers.

The Eagle

The Eagle is a predatory bird: it feeds upon what it can rob, and eats flesh. For it seizes hares, fawns, and geese from the courtyard, and other creatures.

'Zeus's Eagle'

Only the Eagle which is called 'Zeus's bird ' does not touch meat: for it, grass is sufficient. And though it has never heard of Pythagoras of Samos, for all that it abstains from animal food.

9. The Malmignatte and the Asp, their bites

If one merely touches a Malmignatte, it kills, they say, without any violent pain. Moreover Cleopatra established that the bite of an Asp is exceedingly gentle. When as Augustus was approaching she made enquiries at her banquets for a form of death that should be painless:

Death by the sword, she was told, entailed suffering, as was confessed by those who were wounded; death by drinking poison caused distress, for it produced convulsions and pains in the stomach.

Whereas death from the bite of an Asp was gentle. And there are some creatures that kill by a belch those that only touch them, as for instance the Dipsas and the toad.

Listen also to the wiles of the Fox-shark and learn the kind of things it does. Either it will not come near the hook at all, or else it swallows it and immediately turns itself inside out, reversing its body just like a garment, and in this way no doubt it gets rid of the hook.

10. Frogs and their mating

Men say that there are certain spells to cause love; the Frog as a signal for sexual intercourse emits a certain cry to the female, like a lover singing a, serenade, and this cry is called its croak, so they gay. And when it attracts the female to itself they wait for the night.

They cannot copulate under water, and they shun mutual embraces on land in the daytime. But when night descends they emerge with complete fearlessness and take their pleasure of one another. Whenever Frogs utter their cry more loudly and more clearly than is their wont, it signifies that rain is coming.

The Torpedo

I have often heard my mother say, when I was a child, that if a man touches a Torpedo, his hand is seized with the affliction corresponding to its name (torpor). And I have learnt from persons of experience that if a man touches even the net in which it has been captured his entire body is numbed.

And if one throws it alive into a vessel and pours salt water upon it, and if the fish happens to be pregnant and the time of its delivery is at hand, then it gives birth. And if one pours the water in the vessel over a man's hand or foot, the hand or foot is inevitably numbed.

The stings and bites of various creatures

Neither in the stings nor in the bites which they inflict do animals always retain is the same force, but it often augmented from some cause.

For instance, if a Wasp has tasted a viper's flesh its sting is fiercer; and if a Fly has been near something of the same kind its bite is sharper and causes pain; the bite of an Asp too is rendered quite incurable if it eats of a frog.

If a healthy Dog bites a man, it causes a wound and a burning pain, but if the Dog is mad, the bite is deadly. A seamstress was mending a shirt that had been torn by a mad Dog, when she somehow bit it with her mouth in order to stretch the shirt: she went mad and died.

The bite of a human being when fasting is dangerous and hard to cure. And the Scythians are even said to mix serum from the human body with the poison that they smear upon their arrows to drug them. This serum some- how floats on the surface of the blood and they know a means of separating it.Theophrastus is a sufficient witness to the fact.

11. The Snake and its eye-sight

When a Snake sloughs its old skin (it does so at the beginning of spring), then is the time when it purges away the mist over its eyes and the dullness of its sight and what I may call the 'old age' of its eyes; and as it sharpens either eye by rubbing fennel along the edges it rids itself of this affliction.
You see, after hibernating through the winter in some dark hole, it is short-sighted. And so the gentle warmth of the fennel cleanses the creature's vision which the frosts have numbed, and makes its sight keener.

12. The Halcyon and its nest

When the Halcyon realises that it is pregnant it builds itself a nest to receive its brood; but it has no need of mud and a roof and houses, like the swallow which entering as an uninvited guest saddens the dawn with its twitter and even disturbs our slumbers at their sweetest; nor yet does it use its body but its beak alone as it applies itself to the aforesaid task in places away from man.

Weaving together and collecting the spines of the gar-fish, and by some mysterious means it binds together and encloses the fabric of its careful contriving. For some of the bones it fixes upright, others cross-wise (one would say that it was some woman skilled in weaving that was interlacing the woof with the warp), and makes the nest approximately round and bellying in shape, as though it were plaiting a weel.

And when it has woven the aforesaid nest it takes it down to the sea, and there, as the wave's flow gently in, the advancing surf puts the Halcyon's labour to a test. For the water encountering any part that is not watertight penetrates the nest, and the Halcyon seeing this, repairs it. But if you strike with a stone the parts which have been closely fitted, you will not pierce them.

And if you try to cut them with steel, so well and truly have they been inter- woven that they will not yield, any more than that linen corselet which they say Amasis gave as an offering to Athena of Lindus.

And the mouth of this Weel no other creature can enter or indeed detect at all: it admits the Halcyon alone. But not even a drop of sea water could trickle in, so watertight is the nest. And there, they say, rocked on the waves the Halcyon rears its young.

13. The Starfish and Oysters

Starfishes are marine creatures, and they too have a soft shell, but are the enemies of oysters, for they feed on them. And their method of assailing the oysters is as follows. The latter frequently open for coolness sake and anyhow in order to feed themselves on whatever comes their way.

Accordingly the Starfishes insert one of their limbs between the shells and take their fill of the flesh, the oysters being precluded from closing again. So much then for this characteristic of Starfishes.

The herb Wolf's-bane

By the Nile there grows a herb, and it goes by the name of 'Wolf's-bane,' and it is truly named. For when a wolf treads upon it he dies in convulsions. That, you see, is why those Egyptians who worship this animal prevent this herb from being introduced into their country.

Dead bodies in wine and oil

If a bird of the household falls into a vessel of wine and is drowned, they say that neither the wine nor any of the inmates of the house suffers any harm; whereas if it sinks in water, it causes the water to smell, and diffuses a foul odour in the surrounding air.

But if a Gecko falls into wine and is drowned, it does no harm. If however it falls into oil and dies, it makes the oil smell nasty, and on anyone who tastes it lice at once break out.

The 'Thracian Stone'

It is clear that the burning of a Stag's horn expels snakes. And Aristotle asserts that the stone which occurs in the river Pontus (it is in the territory of the Sinti and Maedi) if burnt also chases away snakes.

Moreover he describes the nature of the stone as follows. If you pour some water upon it, it lights; and if when burning you hope to kindle it into a bigger blaze by fanning it, it goes out. They say that as it burns it gives off a smell more oppressive than bitumen. And Nicander agrees with this.

Helen of Troy and Snakes in Pharos

The island of Pharos (what I am about to tell you is reported by the Egyptians) was once infested with a great variety of snakes. But when Thonis the Egyptian King took under his charge Helen the daughter of Zeus (because Menelaus entrusted her to him while he was wandering through Upper Egypt and Ethiopia), he fell in love with her, and when he attempted to force her to lie with him, the story goes that the daughter of Zeus repeated the whole tale to the wife of Thonis (Polydamna was her name), and she on her side, anxious lest this alien should prove more beautiful than she, removed Helen to the safety of Pharos and gave her a herb disliked by the snakes there; so as soon as they were aware of this, the snakes went underground. But Helen planted the herb and in time it flourished and produced seed disagreeable to the snakes, and in Pharos such creatures have never recurred. Experts in these matters say that this herb is called Helenion.

The Amphisbaena

Poets and the compilers of ancient legends, among whom is Hecataeus the chronicler, may sing of the Hydra of Lerna, one of the Labours of Heracles; and Homer may sing of the Chimaera with its three heads the monster of Lycia kept by Amisodarus the Lycian king for the destruction of many, of varied nature, and absolutely invincible.

Now these seem to have been relegated to the region of myths. The Amphisbaena however is a snake with two heads, one at the top and one in the direction of the tail. When it advances, as need for a forward movement impels it, it leaves one end behind to serve as tail, while the other it uses as a head. Then again if it wants to move backwards, it uses the two heads in exactly the opposite manner from what it did before.

14. The Fishing frog

There is, it seems, a species of frog which bears the name of 'Angler,' and is so called from what it does. It possesses baits above its eyes: one might describe them as elongated eyelashes, and at the end of each one is attached a small sphere.

The fish is aware that nature has equipped it and even stimulated it to attract other fish by these means. Accordingly it hides itself in spots where the mud is thicker and the slime deeper, and extends the aforesaid hairs without moving. Now the tiniest fishes swim up to these eyelashes, imagining that the round, swinging objects at the end are edible; meanwhile the Angler lies in wait, never stirring, and when the little fishes are near to him, he withdraws the hairs towards himself (they are drawn in by some secret and invisible means), and the little fishes, whose gluttony has 'brought them close up, provide a meal for the aforesaid frog.

15. Crayfish and Octopus

The Crayfish is the enemy of the Octopus. The reason is this: when the Octopus throws its tentacles round it, it cares nothing for the spines that spring from the back of the Crayfish, but wraps itself round and throttles it till it suffocates.

This hellebore upon it. Now I am in favour of Female-killer, but not at all of white hellebore. The reason is that I detest scorpions but love mankind. Callimachus relates how a tree that goes by the name of yew grows in Trachis, and if creeping things go near and touch it at all they die.

Flesh of the Pig

It is generally believed that the flesh of the Pig is sweeter than all others. And the fact is quite clearly proved by experiment. Whenever it eats a salamander, the Pig itself is unaffected, but kills those who taste its flesh.

Snakes at the source of Euphrates

In what respect the Euphrates, which flows between Parthia and Syria, is superior to other rivers I will explain some other time; but what the Parthians and Syrians know about it, and what is relevant to the present discourse, that I will now tell. Near to the spot where the river first rises certain Snakes breed which are deadly enemies to men, not however to the natives who have been brought up in their midst, but to strangers who have no connexion whatever with them. And they even punish visitors with death.

16. The Lion's tracks

The Lion when walking does not move straight forward, nor does he allow his footprints to appear plain and simple, but at one point he moves forward, at another he goes back, then he holds on his course, and then again starts in the opposite direction.

Next he goes to and fro, effacing his tracks so as to prevent hunters from following his path and easily discovering the lair where he takes his rest and lives with his cubs. These habits of the Lion are Nature's special gifts.

Hiccups and its cure

Consider what makes a good shepherd. Now the herdsman loves both his sheep and his goats, but he abhors the hiccups. This affliction often befalls man, and a surfeit induces hiccups in sheep and goats also.

Accordingly herdsmen plant round the pens of the aforesaid animals a certain herb which counters this complaint, and the herb protects them against it. And those who have had experience maintain that this herb is beneficial to man also in the same affliction.

Henbane, how gathered

Those whose business it is to gather Henbane and the juice of Silphium dig trenches round the plants and stir the roots a little; they do not how- ever pull them up with their hands, but capture or buy some bird and fasten one leg to the herb. And as the bird flutters it pulls up the herb. Both are serviceable to man's needs. But if a man has not these means to pull them up, then the treasure which he fancies he has found so happily and in answer to his needs is of no service

17. The Argonaut

The Argonaut also is one of the polyps and has one shell. Now it rises to the surface by turning its shell upside down to prevent it from taking in salt water and being thrust down again. And when it is on top of the waves, if the weather is calm and the winds are at rest, it turns its shell (which floats like a boat)»0n its back, and letting down two tentacles, one on either side, with a gentle motion rows and propels its natural vessel.

And if there is a wind it extends still further what up till now were oars, using them as rudders, and raises other tentacles between which there is a web of most delicate texture, and this it spreads and turns into a sail; and in this way it navigates so long as it has nothing to fear.

If however it is afraid of some of the larger and stronger fish, it submerges and fills its shell and sinks with the weight of water, and by disappearing escapes from its enemy. Then when it has peace again it rises and resumes its sailing. It is from these activities that it derives its name.

The depth of the sea
They say that men have explored the sea to a depth of 300 fathoms, but not as yet beyond that. Whether there are fishes and animals swimming at an even greater depth, or whether even to them these regions are inaccessible, although the gods of the sea and also the overlord of the moist world have their allotted dwelling there--these are matters into which I shall not enquire too closely, and no one else informs us.

18. The 'Adonis' fish

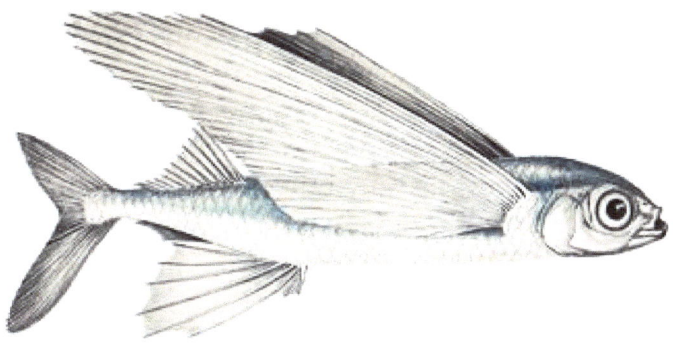

There is, it seems, a fish of the species mullet which is accustomed to live and to feed among rocks, and is yellow in appearance. There are two names for it in common use, for some call it 'Adonis,' others Exocoetus.

For, you see, when the waves are lulled in places where the water is calm and Smooth, it runs aground, borne forward by the force of the wave, and spreading itself upon the rocks, sleeps a deep and tranquil sleep.

And it is well aware that there is peace between it and all other creatures, though it dreads all birds that are or are-reputed to be nurslings of the sea. And so if one appears, the fish leaps up and dances as nature has taught it with movements that, one might say, baffle description, until it jumps off the rock, falls into the sea, and is safe.

People like to call it 'Adonis' because it loves both land and sea, and those who first gave it this name were hinting (so I think) at the son of Cinyras whose life was divided between two goddesses; one who loved him was beneath the earth, the other above.

19. Grafting of trees

A twig of one tree will grow on the stock of another to which it often bears no relation. And Theophrastus, who has traced the cause of this in a thoroughly scientific way, explains the cause small birds eat the blossoms of trees and then as they sit upon the trees void their excrement.
And so the seed dropping into hollows and cracks and cavities, and being watered by the rains of heaven, produces the same wood as that from which it sprang. Thus you will see a fig-tree on an olive-tree, and the same with other trees.

20. The Sea-sheep and others

The Sea-sheep and the Hepatus as it is named, and what fishermen are accustomed to call the Prepon have their lairs in the recesses of the sea. They are of enormous size to look at but sluggish swimmers, and range to and fro around their lairs, and so it comes about that they never abandon their hiding-places. But they lie in Wait for fish of weaker species that swim past. The Hake too may be reckoned as belonging to this class. More than any other fish does it dread the rising of the Dog-Star.

21. Insects, etc, born in plants

It seems that the family of Blister-beetles is produced in fields of wheat and on poplar-trees, and on fig-trees also, as Aristotle says and Caterpillars are produced among peas, and certain Spiders among bitter vetch, and the Leek- cutter as it is called, among leeks.

And in the cabbage is born a kind of worm which derives its name from its habitat. At any rate it is called the Cabbage-caterpillar. The apple-tree also produces a, creature which frequently destroys the fruit of this tree, although it may help women who are still of an age to bear children to conceive. How this happens another shall tell.

Animals know where their strength lies
It seems that every creature knows in which part of its body its strength resides, and this gives it confidence, for when attacking it employs it as a weapon, when in danger as a means of defence.

For instance, the Swordfish defends itself with its snout as with a sword; hence its name; and the Sting-ray with its sting, and the Moray with its teeth, and well it may, because it has a double row of them.

The Mouse

The domestic Mouse is a timorous and feeble creature and is scared by noise and trembles at the squeak of a marten. Field-mice also are timorous, whereas the Sea-mice!' are bolder than the domestic animal.

The 'Sea-mouse'

Though their body is small their courage is irresistible, and this they derive from two weapons, their tough skin and their powerful teeth. And they fight even with fish of greater bulk and with the most skilled fishermen.

The Tunney

The Tunney is aware of the changes of the seasons and knows precisely when the solstices occur and has no need whatsoever of persons skilled in celestial matters. For in Whatever place the beginning of winter overtakes these fish, there they are glad to remain at rest without stirring, and there they stay until the coming of the equinox. Aristotle bears witness to this.

And that they see with one eye and not with the other is admitted by Aeschylus when he says

'Casting his left eye askance like a Tunney.'

And they pass into the Euxine, keeping the land on their right, on which side in fact they look out. Contrariwise when issuing from the Euxine they swim along the opposite shore and hug the land, taking the utmost precaution to safeguard their life by means of the eye which sees.

22. The Common Crab

The first shells of the common Crab splits and, just as snakes slough their 'old age,' so do these creatures put off their shell. And directly they perceive that it is coming away from their flesh they move frantically in every direction in their search for more food, in order that they may become inflated by the additional bulk and so break off their shell.

And when they have contrived to slip out of it and are free, they lie on the sand exhausted like dead bodies. But their growing shell causes them anxiety while it is still rather pliable and tender. Gradually however they gather themselves together and come to life, as it were, and begin by eating sand. But as long as their outer covering consists of membrane, for so long are they timid and utterly lacking in courage.

When however the membrane begins to harden and to assume the nature of a shell, then they cast aside their fears, and the protection of their covering and their full suit of armour, as you might call it, gives them the same confidence as a shield would.

The Troglodytes and Snakes

The race of men known as Troglodytes is famous, and derives
its name from its manner of living. Snakes are afraid of them,
the reason being that the men eat them. Snakes when engaged
in coupling emit a most offensive odour.

The Octopus and fruit-trees

If a field, or if trees with fruit upon them are close by the sea,
farmers often find that in summer Octopuses and Osmyluses
have emerged from the waves, have crept up the trunks, have
enveloped the branches, and are plucking the fruit. So when
they have caught them they punish them. And as quittance for
what the aforesaid fish have reaped they provide the owners
of the pillaged fruit with a feast.

23. The Sea-urchin

If one crushes Sea-urchins while still alive within their shells and with their spines protruding and then throws one bit here and another there into the sea and leaves them, they come together again and join up: they recognise their related fragments, and attaching themselves grow together. And it is by some marvelous and peculiar force of Nature that they become whole again.

The migration of fishes

'Migrants' is the name for marine creatures that are clever at knowing the transition of the Seasons. At any rate at the beginning of winter they escape from the frosts and remain at rest and are glad by so remaining to keep warm, sharing their warmth in brotherly fashion. Then in the spring they begin to swim greater distances and feed not only upon what comes their way but on what they have sought for and tracked down.

Sexual stimulants for animals

With a view to increasing the offspring of their animals their keepers and herdsmen at the mating season take handfuls of salt and of sodium carbonate and rub the genitals of their female asses and goats and mares.

These substances produce in the animals a greater appetite for sexual intercourse. Others rub their parts with pepper and honey; others again with sodium carbonate and nettle-seed. And some have in fact applied Cretan alexanders and sodium carbonate. And from the consequent irritation the females of a herd cannot contain themselves but go mad after the males.

24. The largest of the Cetaceans

There is not one of the largest Cetaceans that Comes near the shore or the beach "or 'leprous' (that is, rocky) spots or into shallow water: they live in the deeps. The largest of them are the Sea-lion, the Hammer-headed Shark, the -Sea-leopard, the great Whales, the Pristis, and the fish called Maltha. This last monster is a terrible antagonist and invincible.

The Ram-fish also is a creature to be dreaded and is dangerous, even if it emerges at a distance, owing to the upheaval in the sea and the wave which it creates. The Sea-hyena too is no auspicious sight for seafarers. As to Sharks, I have spoken above of their different kinds and of their strength.

The Sea-calf

Sea-calves ° are marine animals, and on head lands and projecting rocks they utter a kind of ewe" ominous cry and a very deep roar. And moreover whoever hears this sound, for him there is no escape, but he dies soon after.

The Whale

The Whale too comes out of the sea and warms itself in the sun.

The Seal

But Seals emerge for choice when it is dark, although they do in fact sleep on shore at midday. Homer knew this, and in the Odyssey he has represented Menelaus explaining to Telemachus and Pisistratus this habit they have of resting, when he was telling them of what happened at Pharos and of the sea-god Proteus and of the prophecy which was uttered by the aforesaid Proteus.

Get All The Books In The Series:

Animal Peculiarity Volume 1 [Part 1-8]
Animal Peculiarity Volume 2 [Part 1-8]
Animal Peculiarity Volume 3 [Part 1-8]